Simply Sourdough

·· The Alaska Way ··

By Kathy Doogan

Todd Communications

Anchorage, Ketchikan, Juneau and Fairbanks, Alaska

Simply Sourdough -- The Alaska Way

© 2007 by Todd Communications

Todd Communications
611 E. 12th Ave., Suite 102
Anchorage, Alaska 99501-4603 U.S.A.
Telephone: (907) 274-TODD (8633)
Telefax: (907) 929-5550
Sales@toddcom.com
WWW.ALASKABOOKSANDCALENDARS.COM

With other offices and warehouses in:
Ketchikan, Juneau, & Fairbanks, Alaska

Book Design By:
Kathy Doogan/Raven Design & Cartography

First Printing March, 2007
Second Printing April, 2008
Third Printing June, 2009
Fourth Printing June, 2010
Fifth Printing May, 2013

ISBN: 978-1-57833-960-0
Printed in the United States of America

Additional copies of this book may be ordered directly from the
publisher for US$11.95 (includes US$3 postage & handling).

COVER PHOTO: Klondike miners admire a loaf of freshly-baked
bread. (H.J. Woodside, Library and Archives Canada, PA-016141)

Contents

·· Breads and Rolls ··

·· Cakes, Cookies and Other Desserts ··

Acknowledgements

Creating a cookbook is a group effort. After developing the recipes, each one must be tested and, often, retested. And then they need to be tasted.

This book would have been impossible without the help of a dedicated group of friends and relatives who generously helped me test — and taste — all of the recipes. My sincere thanks go to Cass Crandall, Ruth Ann Dickie, Barbara Doogan, Kaylene Johnson, Susan and Catherine Sullivan, and Jeannie Thompson. Their suggestions led to many refinements to the recipes, and many of their comments have been incorporated into the recipe descriptions and instructions. I must also express my gratitude to all of the tasters — too many to mention by name — who selflessly sampled baked good after baked good, and whose comments also helped these recipes take their final form.

And finally, a special thank you to my husband, Mike, my most enthusiastic taster, for his help and encouragement throughout the project.

— *Kathy Doogan*

A Bit About Sourdough

Sourdough is thought to be the oldest form of leavened bread. Some think it was discovered as long ago as 4000 BC, when Egyptians accidentally left some dough out at room temperature and it picked up wild yeast from the air and began rising. Until commercially produced baking yeast became widely available in the mid to late 19th century, various forms of sourdough provided the primary method of leavening bread.

But mention sourdough today and most people think of gold rushes — prospectors in the California rush of 1849, the Klondike gold rush of 1898 and several that followed in Nome, Iditarod and Fairbanks, Alaska depended on their sourdough. As long as they had their starter and some flour, miners wouldn't go hungry. The treasured starters were passed from person to person, and some were even treated as family heirlooms and passed from generation to generation, especially in Alaska.

Sourdough works when its yeast, either wild organisms from the air or added commercial varieties, gives off carbon dioxide. This gas creates tiny bubbles in the dough, causing it to rise. The yeast feeds on sugar in the dough and converts it to lactic acid, the source of the sour flavor. Different strains of yeast give the starters different flavors. Perhaps the best known is the distinctively sour taste of San Francisco sourdough bread, which one bakery there claims to have been making from the same starter since 1849. Sourdough starter quickly made its way north to the Klondike and Alaska.

Bakers today enjoy using sourdough for the light texture and mild to strong sour flavor it gives baked goods.

Getting Starting With Sourdough

The easiest way to get started with sourdough is to get some starter from a friend or relative. If this isn't an option, there are almost as many recipes and methods for making your own sourdough starter as there are recipes for using it. This book presents three starter options: You can use the packet of starter powder found inside the back cover of this book (just follow the directions on the packet), or you can make your own starter using one or both of the following recipes. Before beginning, read "Tips for Working With Sourdough" on page 9.

Traditional Sourdough Starter
(no added yeast; requires proofing before use)

2 cups warm water
2 cups flour

Place ingredients in a glass bowl and blend well with a wooden or plastic spoon. Cover loosely with a clean towel (this allows air to enter the bowl so your starter can pick up wild yeasts from the environment) and place it in a warm spot. Once a day, remove **half** the starter and throw it away. To the remaining starter, add 1 cup flour and 1 cup warm water; stir in well until most of the lumps are gone. After 3 or 4 days of replenishing the starter it should be bubbly and have a pleasant sour smell. It is then ready to be used immediately or it can be placed in a clean container with loose cover and refrigerated for later use.

Before using this starter, it must be "proofed." To do this, take the starter out of the refrigerator several hours before you plan to use it. Add 1 cup flour and 1 cup warm water; stir well with a wooden or plastic spoon. Cover loosely with a clean towel or plastic wrap and set in a warm place to proof. The starter is ready to use when it becomes frothy and again has a sour smell, anywhere from 2 to 8 hours. (Since proofing time varies so much, if you want to bake first thing in the morning, you should set your starter out to proof overnight.)

Quick and Simple Sourdough Starter
(with yeast; no proofing needed)

1½ cups lukewarm milk (skim or lowfat works best)
¼ teaspoon active dry yeast
1 teaspoon sugar
2 cups all-purpose flour, divided
½ cup water

Place the milk in a glass or plastic mixing bowl; sprinkle with the yeast. Using a wooden or plastic spoon, stir in the sugar and 1½ cups of the flour; mix well to prevent clumps of flour (small lumps are okay). Cover loosely and let sit in a warm place for 3 days. During this time, there should be no need to stir or otherwise disturb the starter.

After 3 days, stir in the ½ cup water and the remaining ½ cup flour. Cover loosely again and leave at room temperature for a minumum of 2 hours and up to 1 day; the mixture should develop bubbles and have a pleasantly sour smell. The starter is now ready to use.

To use your starter, stir well, then remove the amount of starter called for in the recipe and set aside. Replenish the remaining starter by mixing in 1 cup warm water and 1 cup flour for each cup of starter you removed. Pour into a clean glass or plastic container, leaving plenty of room for expansion; cover loosely and store in the refrigerator. Your starter will last virtually forever as long as you use it regularly and replenish it as described above each time you do so.

Sourdough Terminololgy

Hooch: A harmless watery liquid (varying in color from clear or yellow to dark brown) containing alcohol that forms on your starter — most often on the top, but it can form on the bottom.

Proofing: Allowing your starter to ferment and become active.

Sponge: Active starter, ready to use.

Tips For Working With Sourdough

·· Sourdough can react to metal so it is best to avoid metal utensils and bowls when preparing the recipes.

·· **Never** store your starter tightly covered — gas given off by fermentation can cause a tightly sealed container to explode!

·· If the starter forms a layer of liquid on top, don't worry — this is a normal by-product of the fermentation process. Pour off the liquid if the starter is thin, or stir it in if the starter is thick. (The ideal consistency for starter is like thick pancake batter.)

·· How much flour you will need to use in a recipe will depend in part on the thickness of your starter. For the best results, start your recipe using the minimum amount of flour called for (or by holding back ½ cup or so) — you can always add more during kneading if the dough is too sticky.

·· The best environment for letting dough rise is a warm (70° to 80°), draft-free place. If your house is cool and you can't find such a spot, try using your oven: One method is to turn the oven on for about 60 seconds, then turn it off and place the dough in the warm oven to rise. Another method, perfect if your climate is dry as well as cold, is to place a large baking pan on the bottom rack of a cold oven. Fill the pan half-way with boiling water. Place your dough on the top rack and close the door. This creates a warm and moist place for the rise.

·· Starter can be frozen if it won't be used for a long period. Thaw frozen starter at room temperature before using.

A Note on Added Yeast

Some people think that a recipe isn't "true" sourdough if it uses yeast in addition to the starter. For those purists, note that some of the recipes presented here have added yeast and others do not. Adding a small amount of yeast boosts the action of your sourdough and ensures a successful and quicker rise. Any of the recipes in this book can be made with sourdough starter alone, but if omitting yeast, just keep in mind that a dough with yeast added rises in about half the time of one relying only on sourdough.

Notes on Recipe Instructions and Ingredients

·· **Temperatures** given are in degrees Fahrenheit.

·· **Baking times** assume that the oven has been preheated to the appropriate temperature.

·· Unless otherwise noted: **Flour** specified in recipes is white, all-purpose flour; **sugar** is white sugar; **eggs** are large; and **yeast** is active dry yeast.

·· All **ingredients**, including your starter, should be at room temperature unless instructions indicate otherwise.

·· Bread recipe instructions call for kneading by hand, but any of the bread recipes in this book can be made using a standard mixer with a dough hook attachment if desired.

Sourdough
Recipes

Pancakes, Waffles and Other Breakfast Breads

Sourdough Pancakes

This is the simplest and most traditional sourdough recipe.

> 2 cups sourdough starter
> 1 egg
> ¼ cup vegetable oil
> 2 tablespoons sugar
> ½ teaspoon salt
> ½ teaspoon baking soda

Have all ingredients at room temperature. Mix starter, egg and oil in a bowl. Add sugar, salt and soda and mix well. Spoon onto a lightly greased griddle or skillet over medium-high heat. Turn pancakes when surfaces are covered with bubbles. Makes about 12 pancakes.

Sourdough Blintzes

Pancakes:
2 cups sourdough starter
2 eggs
¼ cup vegetable oil
2 tablespoon sugar
½ teaspoon salt
½ teaspoon baking soda

Filling:
1 cup ricotta or cottage cheese* (see note)
1 egg yolk
1 tablespoon sugar
1 tablespoon melted butter
2 teaspoons finely grated orange zest
¼ teaspoon cinnamon
pinch of salt

To make pancakes, mix starter, eggs and oil in a bowl. Add sugar, salt and soda and mix well (batter will be very thin). Using about ¼ cup batter for each, make large (7" to 8" diameter) pancakes on a lightly greased griddle or skillet, preheated to medium heat. Cook until bubbles appear on top and surface looks dry — do not turn over! Remove pancakes from griddle and set aside until all are cooked.

Combine all filling ingredients in a bowl and mix well. Place about a tablespoon of filling in the center of the baked side of each pancake. Fold all four sides over the filling to make an envelope. Place on a greased, preheated griddle, seam side down, and cook over medium heat until brown, turning once. Top with sour cream and/or berries or other fruit, if desired.

Makes about 12 blintzes.

*NOTE: If your cottage cheese contains lots of liquid, let it drain for an hour or two before using by placing it in a collander lined with paper towels and set over a large bowl.

Sourdough English Muffins

This recipe might appear complicated, but once you've made these you'll never go back to store-bought muffins. Split these light-as-a-feather muffins with a fork and toast them, then serve hot with butter and your favorite jam.

   2 teaspoons granulated sugar
   1 teaspoon yeast
   ⅓ cup warm water
   1 cup sourdough starter
   2 to 3 cups flour
   1 tablespoon butter, softened
   1 teaspoon salt
   2 to 3 tablespoons cornmeal (for baking sheet)

In a large mixing bowl, dissolve the sugar and yeast in the warm water. Mix in the sourdough starter and ½ cup of the flour. Set aside in a warm place for 15 to 20 minutes, until bubbles begin to form on the top of the mixture.

Stir in the butter, salt and another ½ cup of flour; beat well. Add as much of the remaining 1 to 2 cups of flour as you need to make a soft dough that holds together and pulls away from the sides of the bowl. Turn the dough out onto a lightly floured surface and knead for 6 to 8 minutes, until it's smooth and springy, kneading in a little more flour only if necessary to prevent sticking. Place dough in a lightly greased bowl, turning to coat all sides. Cover loosely and let rise in a warm place until doubled, 1½ to 2 hours. Gently turn dough out onto a lightly floured board (do not punch down) and let it rest for 10 minutes.

Roll out the dough to ¾" thick. Using a floured 3" or 4" biscuit cutter, cut into rounds. Handling the rounds very gently, place them onto a cornmeal-sprinkled baking sheet. Sprinkle tops generously with additional cornmeal, cover loosely with plastic and let the muffins rise until light, another 1 to 1½ hours.

Using a wide spatula, carefully transfer the rounds to an ungreased frying pan or griddle that has been preheated over medium-low heat. Cook only 4 to 6 at a time, depending on your pan size (don't crowd in pan — muffins should not touch each other). Cook 2 minutes, then carefully turn over so you don't deflate the dough. Cook 2 more minutes; reduce heat to low, then turn again and cook an additional 5 to 6 minutes on each side (14 to 16 minutes total cooking time). When done, the muffins should be golden brown on both sides. Cool muffins on a wire rack.

Makes 8 English muffins. Recipe can be doubled.

Sourdough Waffles

    2 cups sourdough starter* (see note)
    1 teaspoon baking soda
    1 teaspoon salt
    2 tablespoons sugar
    2 eggs
    ¼ cup butter or shortening, melted

In a mixing bowl, combine starter, baking soda, salt, sugar and eggs. Stir in melted butter or shortening. Cook immediately on a hot, greased waffle iron.

Makes about 16 - 4" waffles.

*NOTE: If you do not have enough starter, begin the night before by stirring 2 cups of flour and 2 cups of warm water into your starter. Mix well and leave at room temperature overnight. The next day, remove the 2 cups of starter needed for the recipe and refrigerate the remaining starter.

Sourdough Cinnamon Rolls

1 cup sourdough starter
¾ cup water
3 cups flour, divided
¼ cup vegetable oil
¼ cup brown sugar, firmly packed
2 eggs
1 teaspoon salt
½ teaspoon baking soda
1 teaspoon baking powder
½ cup butter (1 stick), melted

Filling:
1 cup brown sugar
2 teaspoons cinnamon
1 cup chopped walnuts
1 cup raisins

In a large bowl, stir together starter, water and 1½ cups of the flour. Cover loosely and leave at room temperature to proof at least 8 hours (or overnight).

When starter has proofed, mix the oil, sugar and eggs in a small bowl; add to the starter mixture. Stir in remaining 1½ cups flour, salt, baking soda and baking powder. Turn dough out onto a floured board and knead 5 to 8 minutes, or until smooth. Cover loosely and let rest about 10 minutes.

Roll out dough into a rectangle approximately 8" x 18." Brush entire surface with half of the melted butter. In a small bowl, mix filling ingredients; sprinkle evenly over dough. Roll up along the 18" side, forming a log. Using a sharp knife dipped in flour, cut the roll into 12 slices, each about 1½" thick. Dip both sides of slices into remaining melted butter and place in a 9" x 13" baking pan. Set in a warm place and let rise until doubled, 1 to 1½ hours. Bake at 375° for about 40 minutes.

Makes 12 cinnamon rolls.

Sourdough Cake Doughnuts

To ensure success when making these delectable treats, use a candy or deep fat thermometer to keep the temperature of your oil as close to 375° as you can. For deep frying, choose a light-colored oil with a mild flavor, such as canola oil.

1½ cups sourdough starter
2 eggs
¼ cup milk
¼ cup butter (½ stick), melted and cooled slightly
1 teaspoon vanilla extract
1¼ cups sugar
4 cups flour
1 teaspoon salt
2 teaspoons baking powder
2 quarts (approx.) vegetable oil for deep frying

Mix starter, eggs, milk, melted butter, vanilla and sugar in a large bowl. Sift together flour, salt and baking powder and add to the starter mixture; mix thoroughly (dough should be the consistency of a soft biscuit dough). Roll dough out on a floured surface to ½-inch thickness and cut with a well-floured 3" to 4" doughnut cutter (or use a 3" to 4" biscuit cutter to cut rounds, then use a small bottle cap to cut out the holes).

Meanwhile, heat oil to a depth of about 3" or 4" in a large, deep-sided pan to 375°— this can take 15 to 20 minutes over medium heat. Gently lower doughnuts into oil, frying only 3 or 4 at a time — don't crowd pan. Cook until golden brown on both sides, turning once, 2 to 3 minutes total for doughnuts and about a minute for holes.

When done, remove with slotted spoon and drain on racks set over paper towels. If desired, roll warm doughnuts in a mixture of 1 cup sugar and 2 teaspoons cinnamon. Serve immediately.

Makes about 2 dozen 3" doughnuts or 1½ dozen 4" doughnuts.

Sourdough Beignets

These rectangular "doughnuts" are a New Orleans icon. If you want to make beignets for breakfast, the dough can be refrigerated overnight then rolled out, cut and fried the next morning.

1 teaspoon yeast
½ cup warm water
¼ cup sugar
1 cup sourdough starter
½ teaspoon salt
1 egg
2 tablespoons vegetable oil
½ cup evaporated milk
2½ to 3½ cups flour
oil for deep frying* (see note)
powdered sugar for dusting

In a mixing bowl, sprinkle yeast over warm water then stir in 2 teaspoons of the sugar until dissolved. Set aside for about 10 minutes, until small bubbles begin to form. Add the remaining sugar, starter, salt, egg, oil and evaporated milk and mix well. Stir in 1½ cups of the flour and beat until smooth. Add the remaining flour a little at a time until the dough pulls away from the sides of the bowl and becomes too stiff to stir with a spoon. Turn the dough out onto a floured board. Form into a ball and transfer to a clean, lightly greased bowl, turning to coat all sides. Cover with plastic wrap and let rise in a warm place for 1½ to 2 hours. (Or, if desired, cover and refrigerate overnight. The next day, proceed as follows.)

Roll dough to a thickness between ⅛" and ¼", then cut into rectangles about 2" by 3". Heat the oil in a large, deep pot to a depth of 3" or 4" to 360°. Fry the beignets, 3 or 4 at a time, until they puff and become golden on both sides, about 2 to 3 minutes, turning once or twice. Drain on racks set over paper towels. Sprinkle heavily with powdered sugar and serve immediately. Makes about 3 dozen.

*NOTE: In New Orleans, beignets are fried in cottonseed oil, but use any light-colored, mild-tasting oil, such as canola.

Sourdough Blueberry Muffins

1 cup sourdough starter
½ cup vegetable oil
¾ cup water
1 egg
½ cup brown sugar
2 cups flour
½ teaspoon salt
½ teaspoon baking soda
1 cup blueberries, fresh or frozen* (see note)

In a large bowl, stir together starter, oil, water, egg and brown sugar. Sift in flour, salt and baking soda; stir just until combined — do not overmix. Gently fold in blueberries. Spoon batter into greased or paper-lined muffin tins, filling cups ⅔ full. Bake at 375° for 30 to 35 minutes. Makes about 12 large or 18 small muffins.

*NOTE: If using frozen berries, do not thaw before folding in.

Sourdough Corn Fritters

These simple fritters have all the flavor of their traditional, deep-fried cousins without the added fat and mess.

1 recipe Sourdough Pancakes (page 12)
1 cup cornmeal
1½ cups fresh or frozen corn kernels (thawed if frozen)

Prepare the pancake batter; stir in cornmeal and corn kernels. Let the mixture stand at room temperature for about 1 hour. Drop by heaping tablespoons onto a preheated, greased griddle. Cook over medium heat until golden brown, turning once. Serve immediately with butter and maple syrup, if desired. Makes about 3 dozen fritters.

Sourdough Streusel Coffee Cake

1 cup sourdough starter
1 egg
¼ cup vegetable oil
½ cup sugar
1 teaspoon vanilla extract
1 cup flour
½ teaspoon baking soda
¾ teaspoon cinnamon
¼ teaspoon salt
Streusel Topping (recipe below)

In a medium bowl, mix sourdough starter, egg, oil, sugar and vanilla; combine well. Sift together flour, baking soda, cinnamon and salt. Add to starter mixture and stir to combine (don't overmix — a few lumps are okay). Pour into a greased 9" square pan. Sprinkle evenly with streusel topping; bake at 350° for 30 to 35 minutes, or until a toothpick inserted into the center of the cake comes out clean. Serve warm.

Streusel Topping
⅓ cup brown sugar, firmly packed
⅓ cup granulated sugar
2 tablespoons flour
¼ cup cold butter (½ stick), cut into pieces
½ cup chopped walnuts or pecans (optional)

Combine sugars and flour in small bowl. With a fork or pastry blender, cut in the butter until the mixture is crumbly. Add nuts, if using, then sprinkle mixture evenly over batter.

Sourdough Scones

These scones, with a texture much lighter than a traditional scone, are easy to make and perfect with your morning coffee.

> 1 cup flour
> 2 tablespoons sugar
> ½ teaspoon salt
> ¼ teaspoon baking soda
> 2 teaspoons baking powder
> ½ cup (1 stick) cold butter, cut into small pieces
> ½ cup raisins, dried currants or dried cranberries
> 1 egg
> ¾ cup sourdough starter
> 1 tablespoon milk or cream
> 2 tablespoons coarse or raw sugar (for topping)

Into a mixing bowl, sift together flour, sugar, salt, baking soda and baking powder. Cut in the butter with a pastry blender or two knives until the mixture resembles coarse meal. Stir in raisins, currants or cranberries.

Break egg into a 1-cup measure, beat lightly with a fork, then fill the cup with starter (adjust amount of starter if necessary to make mixture equal 1 cup). Add this mixture to the dry ingredients and mix lightly just until combined. Turn out onto a lightly floured board and gently knead 8 to 10 times. Knead in up to ¼ cup more flour if needed to keep dough from sticking (dough should be very soft).

Gently pat dough into a circle about 8" in diameter. Using a floured knife, cut into 8 wedges. Brush tops with milk or cream then sprinkle with coarse sugar. Carefully transfer wedges (use a spatula or pie server) to a lightly greased baking sheet, placing them at least 2" apart. Bake at 400° for 15 to 18 minutes, or until golden. Transfer to a rack to cool slightly before serving.

Makes 8 scones.

Breads and Rolls

Easy Sourdough White Bread

2 teaspoons yeast
1½ cups warm water
1 cup sourdough starter
2 tablespoons sugar
2 teaspoons salt
5 to 6 cups flour
½ teaspoon baking soda

In a large bowl, sprinkle yeast over warm water, set aside for 10 minutes. Add starter, sugar, salt and 4 cups of the flour. Beat well; transfer to a lightly greased bowl, cover loosely and let rise in a warm place until doubled, about 1½ to 2 hours.

Stir baking soda into 1 cup of flour and mix into dough. Turn dough out onto a floured surface and knead, adding more flour if necessary, until dough is smooth and springy (at least 5 minutes). Divide dough in half and form each into a loaf shape. Place in greased 9" x 5" x 3" pans. Cover loosely and let rise again for 1 to 1½ hours. Bake at 375° for about 35 to 40 minutes. Remove from pans and cool on racks.

Makes 2 loaves.

Classic Sourdough French Bread

2 cups sourdough starter
1½ cups warm water
1 tablespoon salt
4 to 5 cups flour

Mix starter, water and salt in a large mixing bowl. Add
4 cups of the flour and mix well. Turn dough out onto a
floured surface and knead until smooth, 5 to 8 minutes,
kneading in as much of the remaining 1 cup of flour as
needed to make a smooth, elastic dough. Put dough in a
lightly greased bowl, turning to coat all surfaces, and place
in a warm spot to rise until double, about 3 to 4 hours.

Punch down dough, turn it out onto a floured surface and
knead again for 1 minute. Divide dough in two; form into
2 oblong loaves and place on a large, greased baking
sheet at least 4 inches apart. With a sharp knife cut 3 or
4 diagonal slits on top of each loaf, then lightly mist the
loaves with water (a clean plant mister works well for this).
Place the loaves in a warm area to rise again until doubled,
another 1½ to 2 hours.

When doubled, place loaves in a 450° oven and mist again
with water. When bread starts to brown, mist the loaves
once more. Bake approximately 20 to 30 minutes total,
or until crust is browned and crispy. Remove loaves from
baking sheet and cool on a wire rack.

Makes 2 loaves.

Sourdough Rye Bread

Because yeast is not effective as leavening for rye flour, rye bread is commonly made with sourdough. This recipe makes a dense, slightly sweet loaf.

> 2 cups sourdough starter
> 3 tablespoons dark molasses
> 2 tablespoons vegetable oil
> 1 tablespoon cornstarch
> ¼ cup water
> 1 teaspoon salt
> 1½ cups rye flour
> 2 tablespoons caraway seeds
> 1 teaspoon baking soda
> 1 cup all-purpose flour

Combine sourdough starter, molasses, oil, cornstarch, water and salt. Stir in rye flour, caraway seeds and soda and blend well. Add the all-purpose flour and knead on a floured surface until smooth, about 5 minutes. Form dough into a ball and place in an oiled bowl, turning to coat all sides. Cover loosely, set in a warm place and let rise until doubled, about 2½ to 3 hours.

Punch dough down and turn out onto a floured board; form into a loaf. Place in a greased 9" x 5" x 3" pan. Brush top lightly with oil. Cover loosely and let rise another 1½ hours. Bake at 375° for 35 to 45 minutes. Remove from pan and cool completely on racks before slicing.

Makes 1 loaf.

Sourdough Whole Wheat Bread

1 teaspoon yeast
½ cup warm water
1 cup sourdough starter
1½ cups whole wheat flour
2 tablespoons dark molasses
2 tablespoons softened butter
1 teaspoon salt
1 to 1½ cups all-purpose flour
½ teaspoon baking soda

In a large bowl, sprinkle yeast over warm water; let stand about 10 minutes. Stir in sourdough starter, whole wheat flour, molasses, butter and salt. Add ½ cup of the all-purpose flour and the baking soda and mix well. Add enough of the remaining flour to make a moderately stiff dough that pulls away from the sides of the bowl.

Turn out onto a floured surface and knead 5 to 8 minutes or until smooth, kneading in additional flour if necessary. Form into a ball and place in a greased bowl, turning to coat. Cover loosely, set in a warm place and let rise 1½ to 2 hours, or until doubled.

Punch dough down and turn out onto a lightly floured surface. Form into a loaf shape and place in a greased 9" x 5" x 3" pan; cover and let rise about 1 to 1½ hours or until doubled again. Bake at 375° for 30 to 35 minutes. Remove from pan and cool on rack.

Makes 1 loaf.

Multigrain Sourdough Bread

¾ cup mixed grains* (see note)
1 cup water
1 cup sourdough starter
2 cups whole wheat flour
1 tablespoon salt
2 tablespoons brown sugar
2 cups all-purpose flour

Put grains into a 1-cup measure; fill to the top with water and allow to soak overnight.

The next day, combine grains with water and starter. Mix in whole wheat flour, salt, brown sugar and 1 cup of the all-purpose flour. On a floured board, knead 8 to 10 minutes, kneading in as much of the remaining 1 cup of flour as needed to make a smooth, non-sticky dough. Place dough in a greased bowl, cover loosely and let rise in a warm place for 3 to 4 hours or until doubled.

Divide dough into 2 equal parts; shape into loaves and place in greased 9" x 5" x 3" pans. Again cover loosely and allow loaves to rise in a warm place for 1 to 2 hours. Bake at 375° for 35 to 45 minutes. Remove bread from pans and cool on a rack.

Makes 2 loaves.

*NOTE: Recipe was tested using equal parts of cracked wheat, rye, oats, millet and flax seeds, but could be made with any combination of grains equalling ¾ cup.

Sourdough Ciabatta (for bread machine)

Because ciabatta requires a very wet, sticky dough to achieve its characteristic airy texture, it is ideal for preparation in a bread machine. This recipe could also be made using a standard mixer with dough hook, but because of the consistency of the dough, kneading by hand is not recommended.

1 cup sourdough starter
¾ cup warm water
1 teaspoon yeast
2 tablespoons extra-virgin olive oil
1½ teaspoons salt
1 tablespoon sugar
1½ cups flour
cornmeal or semolina flour (for dusting baking sheet)

Place all ingredients except cornmeal or semolina flour in the bread pan of your bread machine. Select dough setting and press start. When cycle has finished, dough will be very soft (consistency should be between a batter and a runny dough). Remove dough from pan and place into a large, lightly greased bowl. Cover and let rise in a warm place for 1½ to 2½ hours or until <u>tripled</u> in size (dough will be sticky and full of bubbles).

Prepare a baking sheet by lining with a sheet of parchment paper; sprinkle with cornmeal or semolina flour. Carefully turn the risen dough onto the prepared sheet. Gently pat dough into a rectangle approximately 5" x 10" (be careful not to deflate dough) and dust top with flour. Cover dough loosely and let rise in a warm spot for 1½ to 2 hours.

If you have a baking stone, place it on lowest rack in the oven, set the temperature to 500° and allow the stone to heat for at least 30 minutes. Lower the temperature to 400° and transfer loaf (on parchment paper) to the hot stone. Alternatively, place the baking sheet with loaf on parchment in the oven. Bake for 15 to 20 minutes or until pale golden. Remove from oven and transfer to a wire rack to cool. Makes 1 loaf.

Sourdough Cornmeal-Millet Bread

Millet, a tiny yellow grain, gives this light yet hearty bread a delightfully crunchy texture. Millet should be easy to find in the natural foods section of most supermarkets.

1 teaspoon yeast
¼ cup honey
½ cup warm water
1 cup sourdough starter
2 tablespoons vegetable oil
⅓ cup millet
⅓ cup cornmeal
1 teaspoon salt
3 cups flour

In a mixing bowl, dissolve yeast and honey in warm water; set in a warm spot for about 10 minutes, until mixture becomes bubbly. Add starter, oil, millet, cornmeal and salt; mix well. Stir in 1½ cups of the flour then continue mixing in enough of the remaining flour to make a soft dough that pulls away from the sides of the bowl. Turn out onto a lightly floured board and knead 5 to 8 minutes, until dough is smooth and elastic, kneading in more flour if needed to keep dough from sticking. Form dough into a ball and place in a lightly oiled bowl, turning to coat all sides. Cover loosely and set in a warm place to rise until doubled, about 1½ to 2 hours.

Punch down dough and knead briefly on a floured board. Shape into a loaf and place in a greased 9" x 5" x 3" pan. Cover loosely with plastic wrap and place the loaf in a warm spot to rise for about 1 hour. Bake at 375° for 30 to 35 minutes, or until golden brown. If desired, brush top of hot loaf with about 2 teaspoons of butter. Cool on rack.

Makes 1 loaf.

Sourdough Oatmeal Bread

Oatmeal helps keep this tasty, well-textured bread moist.

1 cup quick-cooking oats
½ cup whole wheat flour
½ cup brown sugar
1 tablespoon salt
2 tablespoons butter or margarine, softened
2½ cups boiling water
1 cup sourdough starter
5 cups all-purpose flour

In a large bowl mix the oats, whole wheat flour, brown sugar, salt and butter. Pour boiling water over mixture, stir to combine and set aside to cool for about an hour. Stir in the starter then add about 4 cups of the all-purpose flour. Turn the dough out onto a floured board and knead for 5 to 8 minutes, kneading in as much of the remaining 1 cup of flour as needed to keep the dough from sticking. Place dough in a lightly greased bowl, turn to coat top, then cover and set in a warm place to rise until doubled, about 3 to 4 hours.

Gently punch down the dough and divide in half. Shape into two loaves and place in greased 9" x 5" x 3" pans. Cover loosely and let rise in a warm spot until doubled again, about 1½ to 2 hours. Bake for 40 to 45 minutes at 350° or until loaves are golden brown and sound hollow when tapped on the bottom of the pan. Remove from pans and cool on rack; brush tops of loaves with melted butter for a softer crust.

Makes 2 loaves.

Sourdough Potato Bread

The recipe for this delicious bread comes from tester Susan Sullivan, who comments that it slices nicely and makes good sandwiches and toast. The recipe uses a standard mixer with dough hook attachment, but it can also be made completely by hand using the general bread-making techniques outlined in other recipes.

2 servings prepared instant mashed potatoes
¾ cup warm milk
¼ cup melted butter
1 cup sourdough starter
2 eggs
2 teaspoons yeast
5½ cups flour, divided
¼ cup sugar
2 teaspoons salt
2 egg whites (for topping)
poppy seeds (for topping)

Prepare mashed potatoes according to package directions; cool to room temperature. In work bowl of mixer, combine potatoes with milk, butter, starter and eggs. In a separate bowl stir together yeast, 2 cups of flour, sugar and salt; add to starter mixture and beat for 2 minutes at medium speed using dough hook attachment. Add 1½ cups more flour, beat for 2 minutes, then add another 1½ to 2 cups of flour and beat to make a stiff dough. Turn dough out onto a floured surface and knead for 8 to 10 minutes; place in a greased bowl, turn to coat, cover loosely and let rise in a warm place until doubled, about 2 hours.

Punch dough down and knead briefly on a floured surface. Divide into 6 pieces and form each into a strip about 1″ thick and 16″ long. Braid 3 strips and form into a loaf, tucking in ends; repeat with remaining 3 strips. Loaves may be set to rise on a large greased baking sheet (for country style loaves) or in 2 greased 9″ x 5″ x 3″ loaf pans. Cover loaves loosely and let rise in a warm place for 1 to 1½ hours. Brush tops of loaves generously with egg whites and sprinkle with poppy seeds. Bake at 350° for 35 minutes. Cool on a rack. Makes 2 loaves.

Rustic Sourdough Bread

The dough for these crusty loaves rises three times, creating a fine, dense texture and full flavor. This bread is best the day it is baked; if you must store it, place it in a paper bag to keep the crust crisp.

¾ cup warm water
1 teaspoon yeast
1 cup sourdough starter
¼ cup milk
1 cup whole wheat flour
2 to 3 cups all-purpose flour, divided
2 teaspoons salt
Cornmeal (for baking sheet)

In large mixing bowl, sprinkle yeast over warm water; stir to dissolve. Add starter, milk, whole wheat flour and 1 cup of the all-purpose flour. Mix well. Cover loosely and let rise in a warm place about 1½ to 2 hours, or until doubled. Stir down, then mix in 1 more cup of all-purpose flour and the salt. Turn dough out onto a floured surface and knead until smooth, 5 to 8 minutes, kneading in as much of the remaining flour as needed to keep dough from sticking. Form dough into a ball; place it in a greased bowl and turn to coat all sides. Cover loosely and set in a warm place to rise until doubled again, about 1 hour.

Gently turn dough out onto a floured board and knead lightly 5 or 6 times. Divide in half; form each into a 3" x 8" loaf. Using a sharp knife, make a shallow cut down the center of each loaf; dust tops with flour. Sprinkle a large baking sheet with cornmeal and place loaves on the sheet, 3" to 4" apart. Cover loosely and let rise once more until doubled, about 1 hour.

Place a large metal baking pan on lowest rack of oven; preheat oven to 500°. Place baking sheet with loaves on rack in lower middle of oven. Immediately pour ½ cup water into the metal baking pan; close oven. Bake 5 minutes then add another ½ cup water to pan. Immediately close door; lower temperature to 425°. Continue to bake until loaves are deep golden brown, about 20 minutes more. Total baking time: 25 to 30 minutes. Remove from baking sheet and cool on racks. Makes 2 loaves.

Sourdough Cinnamon-Raisin Bread

Kids (and adults!) will love this bread toasted or with peanut butter.

1 cup sourdough starter
¾ cup raisins
¾ cup warm water
1 teaspoon yeast
1 tablespoon sugar
1 tablespoon oil
2½ to 3½ cups flour
½ teaspoon cinnamon
¼ teaspoon baking soda
1 teaspoon salt
3 tablespoons sugar
2 teaspoons cinnamon

Mix starter and raisins in a small bowl, cover loosely and allow to proof at room temperature for about 2 hours. (Raisins will become plump and starter will bubble.)

In a large bowl, stir yeast and 1 tablespoon of sugar into the warm water; let stand a few minutes until bubbly. Add the oil, then stir in the proofed starter mixture. Mix in 2½ cups of flour, ½ teaspoon cinnamon, soda and salt. Turn out onto a floured board and knead 5 to 8 minutes, kneading in up to 1 more cup of flour to make a smooth, elastic dough. Form into a ball and place in a lightly greased bowl, turning to coat. Cover and let rise in a warm place until doubled, 1½ to 2 hours.

Punch dough down, turn it out onto a floured board, cover and let rest for 10 minutes. Roll or pat dough into a rectangle, approximately 9" by 12". Sprinkle dough evenly with a mixture of 3 tablespoons sugar and 2 teaspoons cinnamon. Roll up tightly from the 9" side, jellyroll fashion. Pinch ends and place the roll seam side down in a greased 9" x 5" x 3" bread pan. Cover loosely and let rise again for 1 to 1½ hours. Bake at 375° for 30 to 35 minutes. Remove from pan and cool on rack. If desired, brush top of hot loaf with butter for a soft crust.

Makes 1 loaf.

Sourdough Dinner Rolls

1 cup sourdough starter
1 cup warm water
1 teaspoon yeast
2 teaspoons salt
2 tablespoons sugar
2 tablespoons olive oil
3 to 4 cups flour

In a large mixing bowl combine starter, water, yeast, salt, sugar and oil. Stir in 2 cups flour. Add remaining flour a little at a time until dough becomes too stiff to stir. Turn out onto a floured surface and knead 5 to 8 minutes, until smooth and elastic. Place dough in a greased bowl, turn to coat and cover loosely with plastic wrap. Put in a warm place to rise until doubled, about 1½ to 2 hours.

When double, punch dough down and turn out onto a floured surface. Divide into 24 pieces, shape into balls. Place at least 2" apart on well greased baking sheets. Roll balls so all sides of dough are lightly greased. Cover loosely and let rise again until doubled, about 1 hour. Bake at 375° approximately 20 minutes.

Makes 24 rolls.

Sourdough Cheese Rolls

These light and fluffy rolls make a perfect accompaniment to soup or chili. Try making them with different types of cheese, such as Pepper Jack or a smoked Gouda.

1 teaspoon yeast
¾ cup warm water
1 cup sourdough starter
¼ cup sugar
¼ cup butter or margarine, softened
1 egg
2 teaspoons salt
½ teaspoon baking soda
1 cup (about 4 ounces) shredded cheddar cheese
4 to 4½ cups flour

In a large bowl dissolve yeast in warm water; let stand a few minutes until mixture bubbles, then mix in the starter, sugar, butter, egg, salt, baking soda, cheese and 3½ cups of the flour. Mix well then turn out onto a floured board and knead for 5 to 8 minutes, kneading in enough of the remaining 1 cup of flour to make a soft dough. Place in lightly greased bowl; turn to coat top. Cover loosely and let rise 1½ to 2 hours, until double. Punch down, turn out onto a floured board, cover loosely and let the dough rest for 10 minutes.

Divide dough into 24 pieces; with oiled hands, shape into balls and place at least 2" apart on greased baking sheets. Cover loosely with plastic wrap and let rise again until double, about 30 to 45 minutes. Bake at 375° about 20 minutes.

Makes 24 rolls.

Sourdough Kaiser Rolls

These big, puffy rolls are perfect for sandwiches and make great hamburger buns.

2 to 3 cups flour
¼ cup warm water
1 teaspoon yeast
1 teaspoon salt
3 tablespoons sugar
2 eggs
1½ cups sourdough starter
cornmeal (for baking sheet)

Sprinkle yeast over warm water in a small bowl; let stand about 10 minutes, until small bubbles form. Sift 2 cups of the flour, salt and sugar into a large bowl. Add yeast mixture, eggs and starter; mix well. Add as much of the remaining flour as you can stir in; turn dough out onto a well floured board and knead for about 5 minutes, until smooth and elastic, kneading in additional flour if needed to prevent sticking. Place dough in a lightly greased bowl, cover loosely and set in a warm spot until doubled in bulk, 1½ to 2 hours.

Turn dough out onto a floured board, knead 8 ot 10 times, then pat or roll dough out about ¾" thick. Let dough rest about 10 minutes, then cut with a floured biscuit or round cookie cutter 3½" to 4" in diameter. With your finger, poke a hole in the center of each round (do not widen holes — they are supposed to close up again during rising and baking). Place rounds at least 2" apart on baking sheets generously dusted with cornmeal to prevent sticking. Cover loosely and let rise until light and puffy, about 1 hour.

Bake at 375° for 20 to 25 minutes, until golden brown. Cool completely on racks.

Makes about 12 rolls.

Sourdough Garlic-Parmesan Bread Sticks

1 cup sourdough starter
¾ cup water
1 teaspoon yeast
2 tablespoons olive oil
2 teaspoons salt
2 to 3 cloves garlic, finely minced
2 to 3 cups flour
2 teaspoons olive oil
1 cup grated Parmesan cheese

Combine starter, water, yeast, 2 tablespoons olive oil, salt and garlic in a bowl. Stir in 1 cup of flour. Continue adding flour until dough becomes too stiff to stir. Turn out onto a lightly floured board and knead until smooth. Place dough in a greased bowl, turn to coat surface, then cover and set in a warm spot to rise until doubled, about 1½ to 2 hours.

When doubled, punch dough down, knead 8 to 10 times, then let dough rest for about 10 minutes. Pat out dough on a floured surface about ½" thick; brush top with 2 teaspoons of olive oil. Using a floured knife or pizza cutter, cut into strips about ¾" wide and 6" long. Place Parmesan cheese in a shallow dish; roll strips in cheese and place about 1" apart on a greased baking sheet. Cover loosely and let rise in warm area for about 30 to 45 minutes. Bake at 400° for 15 to 20 minutes or until golden brown.

Makes about 24 bread sticks.

Sourdough Gold Nugget Biscuits

2 cups flour
½ teaspoon baking soda
1 teaspoon salt
1 teaspoon baking powder
½ cup (1 stick) cold butter, cut into small pieces
1 cup sourdough starter
½ cup buttermilk
3 tablespoons butter, melted

In a bowl combine flour, soda, salt and baking powder. Cut in butter with pastry blender until mixture resembles coarse meal. In a small bowl, combine starter and buttermilk, then mix into butter and flour mixture with a fork to form a soft dough. Turn out onto a floured board; knead lightly for 30 seconds.

Roll out to ½" thick and cut with 3" cutter. Place on a greased baking sheet and brush tops with melted butter. Cover loosely with plastic wrap and put in warm place to rise for 30 to 45 minutes. Bake at 425° for 12 to 15 minutes or until golden. Serve immediately.

Makes about 15 biscuits.

Sourdough Corn Bread

Sourdough gives this old standard a light, tender texture.

1½ cups flour
½ cup sugar
¾ cup cornmeal
1 tablespoon baking powder
½ teaspoon salt
1 cup sourdough starter
1 cup milk
2 eggs
½ cup vegetable oil or melted butter

Combine flour, sugar, cornmeal, baking powder and salt in medium bowl. In a separate bowl, mix starter, milk, eggs and oil or melted butter; add to flour mixture and stir just until combined (do not overmix). Pour into a greased 9" square pan. Bake at 350° for 30 to 35 minutes, or until golden brown and a toothpick inserted in center comes out clean. Cool pan on rack at least 10 minutes before cutting. Serve warm.

For muffins: Grease or line 18 muffin cups with paper liners. Fill cups ⅔ full with batter; bake at 350° for 18 to 20 minutes.

Basic Sourdough Focaccia

1 cup sourdough starter
½ cup warm water
1 teaspoon yeast
1 tablespoon sugar
¼ cup olive oil
2 to 2½ cups flour
1 teaspoon salt
3 tablespoons olive oil (for topping)
2 teaspoons sea salt or coarse kosher salt (for topping)
1 teaspoon dried rosemary (for topping; optional)

In a large bowl, mix starter, warm water, yeast and sugar. Leave at room temperature 1 to 2 hours, until mixture is bubbly. Stir in olive oil, flour and salt; mix well. Turn dough out onto a floured board and knead until smooth, kneading in more flour if needed to prevent sticking (dough should be soft). Roll dough into a ball and place in an oiled bowl, turning to coat all sides. Cover loosely and place in a warm place to rise until doubled, about 2 hours. Punch down dough and turn it out onto a large, greased baking sheet. Gently pat the dough into a rectangle about 8" by 12". With your fingertips, make "dimples" all over the dough; cover loosely and let rise again in a warm spot for 1 hour. Brush top with olive oil, letting the oil pool in the dimples, then sprinkle on the salt and rosemary, if using. Bake at 375° for 30 to 35 minutes or until golden brown. Serve warm.

Sourdough Focaccia Margherita

Prepare dough for Basic Sourdough Focaccia, omitting the coarse salt and rosemary. Instead, top with the following:

2 tablespoons fresh basil, sliced into thin ribbons
1 large or 2 small Roma tomatoes, thinly sliced
¼ cup grated Parmesan cheese

Bake at 375° for 25 to 30 minutes or until golden brown.

Cakes, Cookies and Other Desserts

Sourdough Chocolate Cake

½ cup butter (1 stick), softened
1 cup sugar
2 eggs
4 ounces semisweet baking chocolate, melted
1 cup sourdough starter
¾ cup milk
1 teaspoon vanilla extract
1¾ cups flour
1 teaspoon baking soda
½ teaspoon salt

Before beginning, be sure starter, milk and eggs are at room temperature. Cream butter and sugar until light and fluffy. Beat in eggs and melted chocolate. Add sourdough starter, milk and vanilla and mix well. Sift together flour, baking soda and salt and fold into batter, mixing until smooth.

Pour batter into a greased 9" x 12" pan or 2 greased 8" round cake pans. Bake at 350° for about 40 minutes for 9" x 12" pan or about 25 minutes for 8" round pans, or until a toothpick inserted in the center comes out clean. Cool, then frost as desired.

Sourdough White Cake

Decorate this cake with your favorite frosting, or try serving it topped with sliced strawberries and whipped cream.

1 cup sugar
½ cup butter (1 stick), softened
2 eggs
2 teaspoons vanilla extract
1½ cups flour
1 teaspoon baking powder
½ teaspoon baking soda
½ teaspoon salt
1 cup sourdough starter
½ cup milk

In a large bowl, cream together the sugar and butter using an electric mixer. Beat in the eggs, one at a time, then add the vanilla and beat on high speed until light and fluffy. In a medium bowl, sift together the flour, baking powder, baking soda and salt; set aside. In another bowl combine the starter and milk. Add about half of the dry ingredients and half of the starter mixture to the sugar, butter and egg mixture and mix well. Add remaining dry ingredients and remaining starter mixture; scrape down sides of bowl, then beat on high speed for about 2 minutes or until batter is smooth. Pour batter into a greased and floured 9" square pan.

Bake at 350° for 35 to 40 minutes, or until cake springs back when pressed gently in the center.

For cupcakes: Spoon batter into 12 cupcake tins lined with paper liners. Bake 20 to 25 minutes.

Sourdough Gingerbread

The addition of sourdough gives this rich, spicy cake a surprisingly light texture.

½ cup brown sugar, firmly packed
½ cup shortening or butter, softened
½ cup dark molasses
1 egg
1½ cups flour
1 teaspoon baking soda
½ teaspoon salt
1 teaspoon ground ginger
1 teaspoon cinnamon
½ teaspoon ground nutmeg
½ teaspoon ground cloves
¾ cup hot water
1 cup sourdough starter
whipped cream (for serving; optional)

In a large mixing bowl, cream brown sugar and shortening or butter until light and fluffy. Add molasses and egg and beat until well combined. Sift flour, baking soda, salt, ginger, cinnamon, nutmeg and cloves into a small bowl; stir in hot water. Pour this mixture into the sugar and egg mixture, blending well. Slowly add the sourdough starter, mixing gently. Pour batter into a greased 9″ square pan. Bake at 375° for 30 to 35 minutes or until a toothpick inserted in the center comes out clean.

Serve while still warm, topped with a dollop of whipped cream if desired.

Sourdough Carrot Cake

1½ cups vegetable oil
2 cups sugar
1 cup sourdough starter
3 eggs
1 (20-ounce) can crushed pineapple, drained
2 cups shredded carrots
½ cup chopped nuts
½ cup shredded coconut
2 teaspoons vanilla extract
2½ cups flour
½ teaspoon salt
1 teaspoon baking soda
2 teaspoons cinnamon
Cream Cheese Frosting (recipe below)

Mix together oil and sugar. Add starter and eggs, one at a time, beating well after each. Fold in pineapple, carrots, nuts, coconut and vanilla. Sift together flour, salt, baking soda and cinnamon; add to the starter mixture and blend well. Pour batter into greased and floured 9" x 13" pan. Bake at 350° for 45 to 50 minutes or until toothpick inserted in center comes out clean. Cool and frost with Cream Cheese Frosting.

Cream Cheese Frosting
8 ounces cream cheese, softened
¼ cup (½ stick) butter, softened
1 pound confectioners sugar (3½ to 4 cups)
1 teaspoon vanilla extract
1½ tablespoons milk

Combine all ingredients, beating until smooth.

Sourdough Chocolate Chip Cookies

Sourdough gives these cookies a much lighter texture than traditional chocolate chip cookies.

> 1 cup butter (2 sticks), softened
> 1½ cups sugar
> 1 teaspoon vanilla extract
> 2 eggs
> 1 cup sourdough starter
> 2½ cups flour
> 2 teaspoons baking soda
> 1 teaspoon baking powder
> 1 teaspoon salt
> 2 cups (12 ounces) semisweet chocolate chips
> 1 cup chopped walnuts or pecans (optional)

Cream butter and sugar until light and fluffy; add vanilla and eggs, mixing well, then stir in the starter. Sift together flour, baking soda, baking powder and salt; add to creamed mixture. Fold in the chocolate chips and nuts, if using. Drop by rounded spoonfuls onto ungreased baking sheets.

Bake at 375° for 10 to 12 minutes. Remove cookies from baking sheets and cool on wire racks. When cool, store tightly covered.

Makes about 5 dozen cookies.

Sourdough Sugar Cookies

The addition of sourdough creates a soft, tender cookie. Be sure dough is well chilled before you try to roll it out.

¾ cup butter (1½ sticks), softened
1 cup sugar
2 eggs
1 teaspoon vanilla extract
½ cup sourdough starter
3 cups flour
½ teaspoon baking soda
1 teaspoon salt
Powdered Sugar Frosting (recipe below)

In a large bowl, cream butter and sugar. Add eggs and vanilla extract and beat until mixture is fluffy, then stir in sourdough starter. In a separate bowl, sift together flour, baking soda and salt; stir into sourdough mixture. Wrap dough in plastic wrap and refrigerate at least 3 hours or overnight.

On a lightly floured board, roll dough to ¼" thick; cut with cookie cutters and place on lightly greased baking sheets. Bake at 350° for 12 to 15 minutes, until light brown. Carefully remove cookies from baking sheets and cool on wire racks. When cool, frost with Powdered Sugar Frosting. Store tightly covered.

Makes about 3 dozen cookies.

Powdered Sugar Frosting
2 cups powdered sugar
½ teaspoon vanilla extract
2 tablespoons butter, melted
2 to 3 tablespoons milk

Mix powdered sugar, vanilla and melted butter with enough milk to make frosting proper spreading consistency. Add a few drops of food coloring if desired.

Sourdough Brownies

The sourdough adds a slight tang to the rich chocolate taste of these brownies.

4 ounces semisweet baking chocolate
½ cup hot water
1 teaspoon baking soda
1 cup (2 sticks) butter, softened
2 cups sugar
2 eggs
2 teaspoons vanilla extract
1 cup chopped walnuts or pecans
1½ cups flour
½ teaspoon salt
1½ cups sourdough starter

Place chocolate in small saucepan and add hot water; bring slowly to a boil, stirring constantly to prevent burning. As soon as chocolate it melted, remove from heat and add baking soda; stir well (mixture will be bubbly). Set aside to cool to lukewarm.

In a large bowl, cream butter and sugar until light and fluffy. Add eggs and vanilla and mix thoroughly. Stir in cooled chocolate mixture and nuts. Sift flour and salt and gradually add to the chocolate mixture, stirring well. Stir in the sourdough starter and mix well. Pour batter into a greased and floured 9" x 13" pan. Place pan in a warm spot for 30 to 45 minutes to rise slightly. Bake at 350° for 35 to 40 minutes. Cool completely before cutting.

Makes 24 brownies.

Sourdough Zucchini Bread

1 cup sourdough starter
2 cups sugar
3 eggs
2 cups shredded zucchini
1 cup vegetable oil
2 teaspoons vanilla extract
2½ cups flour
1 teaspoon baking soda
1 teaspoon salt
2 teaspoons cinnamon
½ teaspoon nutmeg
1 cup chopped nuts (optional)

In a large bowl, combine starter, sugar, eggs, zucchini, oil and vanilla. Sift the dry ingredients together; add to starter mixture and stir well. Stir in nuts, if using. Spoon batter into 2 greased and floured 9" x 5" x 3" loaf pans.

Bake at 350° for 1 hour or until a toothpick inserted in center comes out clean. Let cool in pans for 10 minutes; remove and cool on racks at least 30 minutes before slicing.

Makes 2 loaves.

Sourdough Friendship Bread

This recipe makes 2 loaves so you can share a loaf of this delicious, sweet bread with a friend.

1 cup sourdough starter
1 cup vegetable oil
½ cup milk
3 eggs
2 cups sugar
2 teaspoons vanilla extract
2 cups flour
1½ teaspoon baking powder
½ teaspoon baking soda
½ teaspoon salt
1 teaspoon cinnamon
1 large box of vanilla instant pudding mix* (see note)
1 cup chopped pecans
⅓ cup sugar (for topping)
1 teaspoon cinnamon (for topping)

In a large bowl, combine the starter, oil, milk, eggs, sugar and vanilla; mix well. In a separate bowl, sift together flour, baking powder, baking soda, salt, 1 teaspoon cinnamon and the pudding mix. Add dry ingredients to starter mixture and stir to combine. Stir in pecans.

Grease two 9" x 5" x 3" loaf pans. Combine ⅓ cup of sugar and 1 teaspoon of cinnamon in a small bowl. Sprinkle about a tablespoon of this mixture evenly over the bottom of each greased pan. Pour in batter; sprinkle tops with remaining cinnamon sugar. Bake at 325° for 1 hour or until a toothpick inserted in the center comes out clean. Cool on racks.

Makes 2 loaves.

*NOTE: You can experiment with different flavors of pudding mix such as chocolate or butterscotch.